T0380646

Wait; What Just Happened?

Words by Ryan Miller
Illustrations by Gunnar Miller

To order additional copies of this book, contact:
Xlibris
844-714-8691
www.Xlibris.com
Orders@Xlibris.com

Library of Congress Control Number: 2024905605
ISBN: Softcover   979-8-3694-1819-2
           Hardcover   979-8-3694-2139-0
           EBook   979-8-3694-1818-5

Print information available on the last page

Rev. date: 05/06/2024

CONTENTS

ABOUT THE AUTHOR

Hi, I'm Ryan! I was born in Germany to humble and loving parents from the Midwestern United States. My dad was an Air Force Lt. Colonel, which provided him and my mom a lot of travel and a variety of cultural experiences, which they shared with me. I grew up loving sports and excelling in academics as a scholar athlete who graduated High School with Honors. In school, I gravitated toward the arts such as drama and English versus math and science. Although I hold a Masters Degree in Business Administration, a Bachelors Degree in University Studies, and a Minor in Business Management, I pride myself most on being human and being able to relate to people from a wide variety of lifestyle backgrounds and demographics. In many ways, I place more value in my life experiences than in my formal education. My kids Luke (16) and Gunnar (7) are my pride and joys and we call Las Vegas, Nevada our home.

INTRODUCTION

My goal with these poems is to provide a glimpse into my life in 2023 and to be thought provoking and relatable. Although some writings may seem to point to something in particular, there's a lot that I've left intentionally unsaid to allow for interpretation by the reader. This project is a collection of thoughts that I think many adults, particularly single parents, can relate to on some level. I've included some illustrations by my youngest son, Gunnar, to add some visual insight into his life and relatively innocent experiences as it parallels my often heavier, more jaded experiences... while him and I travel through nearly identical physical spaces and moments in time.

Statistics show that over half of all marriages end in divorce. However, second and third marriages have even higher divorce rates. With this being said, there's a pretty high chance that the person reading this has either been divorced or has a partner who has. Some reports suggest that divorced people are more likely to die earlier than married people, with divorced men dying faster and at a higher rate than divorced women. If this information isn't concerning and intriguing to you, I hope that it at least provides some context and normalization for single and/or co-parenting in 2023. This is one perspective that I bring with these poems as I am a single (divorced) dad of two who is simply pushing to be my best for myself and my boys.

In contrast to my perceived ups and downs as I navigate life, I admire my two sons (Gunnar and Luke) as they seemingly carry on unbothered... like champs. They have a consistent and resilient pace. I'm certain they aren't unaffected, but their ability to persevere with champion mindsets is extraordinary. I celebrate their love for life and willingness to see things in opportunistic, beautiful, and uplifting ways. They often, unknowingly, encourage me to be better, do better, and think better. They fuel me on good and bad days as I do my best to provide for them and more than that... to leave a legacy that they would be proud of.

RAW

Fell in love with art.
Felt destined to share my part.
Impart some of my point of view.
Indulge inner ideas and be one of few.
We're all just a little bit mad.
We all understand it's nothing bad.

SPRING FORWARD

A fluttering butterfly...
Rays of hopeful sunshine...
A snow capped mountain in the distance...
Cold stark reminders of the dark winter gone by.
New life is blooming with each fresh, vibrant spring petal.
It's time to spring forward with vigor and purpose.
It's time to shed the cloudy, pessimistic life-sucking fog of yesterday.
Let's launch into newtopia with clear visions of the next life that's arrived.

RESURRECT

It is finished and so it has started.
It is done and so it's begun.
Without endings, it's not possible to welcome beginnings.
Without death, we can't open our eyes and heart to new life.
Who's to say that this valley doesn't lead to my paradise?
Who's to doubt that here and now isn't my yellow brick road to destiny?
Breathe in peace.
Breathe out life.
It is finished and so it has started.
It is the time to fade.
Fade into now.

STARS (HAIKU I)

Starlit skies above
Home sweet home lies just below
Gazing in full flow

UNTITLED

As I sit on this couch, I can sense the stories it's absorbed over time. If this couch could speak, it would recall long sleepless damp nights of flowing emotions, short lived moments of intense romantic encounters, and afternoon bonding sessions disguised as floating seconds of silent companionship.

Does everything really eventually fade?

The sunlight dances off mirrors and lights flicker in from the window attempting to allow a memory or two to dance on the wall... to the beat of this speaker.

Is anything here to stay after all?

HANG ON

Grip the edge and take a peak.
The scene is all too familiar for comfort.
No stomach drop or palm sweat tells the tale.
Yet another wander into the unattractive magnetizing bleak.
Just takes a minor scale adjustment to stay sharp.
The choices are there to brace for a fall or hit a new trail.
Hints of mint, sugar, and lavender stir the senses as if to beg me to reminisce of paths already ventured.
Relax the grip and embrace the steady heartbeat that's nonchalantly continuing on.
And the beat goes on.
The sun sets and rises again, seemingly unbothered by the twists and turns of the million beaten paths below.

FLUTTER FLUTTER

Fluttering and fluttering...
You float away;
You blow back.
The shifting winds...
The changing tides;
High and low;
Above and below.
Gusts continue to shift...
Metamorphosis is instant.
Adapting and blending randomly;
Seasons come and go.
A human mind is so...
Bounding through obstacles;
Getting through and not over.
Flying brings grand views...
Sitting brings rest and meditation.
The colors of life blend and burst.
Days break and nights bust.
Transitions bring uncertainty.
Hope is wrapped in unknown.
Cheers to the journey...
Courage to the weary;
Love for all mankind.
May you flutter flutter with a head lacking clutter...

UNJADED

Not much compares to your youthful, innocent, true joy.
Life flows through you and happiness is exhaled.
The journey ahead is fluid, regardless of the diabolical.
Nature lends itself to stresses but they're jaded reflections.
Expectations are mixed with unrealized dreams and fake emotions are coated with sugar and ayahuasca roots.
Systematic pressures hide within a pipe dream.
Architect your own path and allow it to unfold, with each newly traversed step.
When life takes you into the heavily traveled areas, emerge leading your own pack.
Invent.
Excel.
Create.
Accelerate.
Be yourself unapologetically and live life forever fulfilled...
Unjaded.

SHARDS

Inflicted pains of yesterday...
They're not here to stay.
Regardless, they stick and stab.
Like, what else can you grab?
Take it all and jet.
You're leaving? Bet.
If I'm the glass... a pane;
You're a shard... not sane.
Pushing back like true love does,
I'm spotting streaking white doves.
It's not about the stress...
or even your little black dress.
When true love is merely a verb,
sometimes the future is a curb.

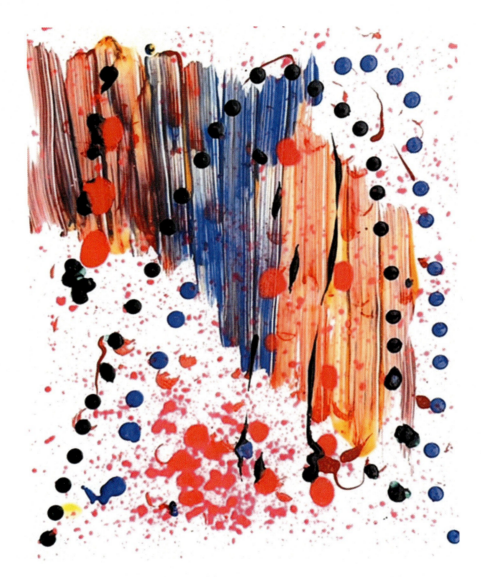

MAD HATTER (HAIKU II)

Brush, splitter, splatter
Reaching depths like a mad hatter
Sharing brain matter

FAINT LIGHT

In the city of lights...
Neon dreams are crushed by cold dice and females are distracted by things much shinier.
Darkness abounds.
Where there's darkness though, there's a light that will overcome.
There's a light beaming to the sky and beyond, like the Luxor on a clear night.
This little light of mine...
I'm going to let it shine.
Sometimes it may be faint,
but at least I know what I ain't.

VISIONS OF VISIONS

Seeing double.
Seeing triple.
My sight is blurry.
I'm clearly squinting.
The yearning takes a toll.
Wait, is that a vision?
It's quite possibly a vision of a vision that passed in the past.
Or this is the newly tweaked version of the previously envisioned vision?
Regardless, I see it.
It's glaring back at me like a hopeful taunt, a loving diss, or an encouraging joke.
It could be an encouraging joke with degrading tendencies.
I'm staring into the distance through a mirror... that's full of lost memories refracting light toward the unknown in front of me.
Visions lend to visions of more visions and visionaries, don't you see?

PASSING SMILES

A momentary feeling of satisfaction filled with uplifting vibes of dopamine.
Happiness is often a short lived experience that is passionately pursued.
When the smiles rush over us, it's never as grand or everlasting as we dreamt it to be.
Desire for more consumes us and we explore how to attract it again and again.
Passing smiles with childlike hope that the saying "what goes around comes around" will prove to be true.
Do work, karma.
"Show your face" we scream and shout!
"Present your faith" echoes back.
Deal a smile today.
Deal one to yourself too.
Pass smiles, even during trials...

MATES IN THE ROOM

Hanging around like bees on spring flowers...
Your presence is constant like the rising and setting of the sun.
Thoughts go unshared and I ponder what you'd like to reveal about where you've been, what you've seen, and the things you've heard.
A lifetime experience as a wallflower;
Yet, I'm certain you live and carry epic stories to tell over a fire pit and a long, dark night.
Although you've been moved, you haven't denied physics to actually move.
Late night conversations are shared, but they feel one sided and leave a feeling of empty curiosity.
Here's to being seen.
Cheers to my roommates.
May your life be creatively yours and one of eternal fulfillment...

LOADING

Booting up,
Powering on,
Loading,
Restarting,
Power cycling,
Rebirthing.
Planet Earth and all of humanity faces the continual battle of charging and recharging...
Physically, mentally, and even literally.
Sands of time flow as moments drift away into history books, lost memory banks, and old
file drawers.
Thoughts of joy and anticipation overcome us as we look toward the sunrises and sunsets we
firmly believe to be yet ahead.
Today slowly slips away as we add to calendars of tomorrow.
For a second, we stop and breathe in the smells of gifts from today that we've yet to recognize
with gratitude.
Coffee,
Food,
Candles,
Quiet Shelter,
Music,
Birds,
Car engines.
The day is loading as we rush to continue our story...

360

Rays of gold pour into the windshield as the car streaks down 215.

Heat intensifies as an over zealous summer enters with strong intentions to leave spring in the rear view of 2023.

Earth spins and new seasons bring new life as hotter weather ushers in a temp gauge of 90.

Staying in drive is a must while facing forward with acceptance that each shift is integral to the journal of life that is 1.

Passing Sunset, I cruise toward some spectator time with my speedometer reflecting an efficient 72.

Tasks and obligations give way to time as the days buzz by and I strive to give 100.

New goals light the soul as I work on enjoying the moments and set my perspective to 20/20.

ME + YOU (HAIKU III)

Eyes of all kinds
Open, shut, dialed, and styled
Two making a pair

RE-ROUTING THE TRIP

Winding streets carry travelers from point A to point B.
At times, there's an additional point C or point D.
Paths curve and flow with the contours of the Earth.
The journey is never straight, starting from birth.
Hiccups, accidents, spills, wrecks, traffic jams, and animals create alterations to plans.
Maps get rearranged and new routes are marked with crayons.
Coloring a new way to reach the destination seems relatively easy.
If only all life alterations or new alignments were this breezy.
Shifting mindset and facing the obstacles is half the war.
Belief and grit that is rooted deep within your core is mandatory to obtain the good that's in store.
Although the destination grabs our focus on what's around the bend,
The trip itself is what must be enjoyed until the end.

SPLIT DECISIONS

Heartache torments and emotions are at high tide.

Blood speeds through the veins and eyes are blinded of current realities by swelling liquids of falsehood.

I wish it were in my power to simply shake you and wake you from this altered state.

Life temporarily bursts into flames and the fiery cannonballs catapult into surrounding people and places that were so valued just hours ago.

My chest tightens and my mind races in desperate attempts to join you where you're at, if only for a split second to possibly pick you up and carry you out.

Weather patterns proceed, clock hours continue, and events carry on.

Your world stops and you unknowingly pick a desolate tunnel to temporarily live in.

I recommit to the decision to be here, in sickness and in health, and position myself patiently at the tunnel's end.

IS IT ME?

Bonds as old as time...
Through golden hours, grit, and grime.
Desolate valleys to blue skies...
Overcoming hurt and blatant lies.
At times questioning "is it you?"
Hollow echoes hit back "yes, and you too."
Wait, you're saying it's me?
Hold on, just let it be.
Committed as Picasso was to art,
we're together and each of us plays a part.
One can't live without the other.
We're like conjoined twins, obsessed lovers, or close brothers.
Yesterday, this wasn't me.
Today, you're all I see.
Are you possibly me 2.0?
Leave, scram, you gotta go.
Questioning all that I am...
Usually I care, but sometimes I don't give a damn.
Is it me?
Or is it me?
Yes, it's me.
Maybe even all three.

2023

In this burning world of the fake, quick videos of heaven on Earth are dealt to the masses.

Quick snaps are shared with cute reassuring captions.

Seldomly caught candid photos are clicked on and deleted quicker than you can say cheese.

Orchestrated selfies are produced on pocket sized devices that carry out self proclaimed lives in them.

Social accounts are built, edited, monitored, and shared.

They're rebuilt, deleted, and remembered.

Pictures are triple filtered to be placed into virtual reality with their carefully chosen audience.

Of course, they're first cropped, chopped, and tagged.

It's no wonder long lasting and loyal relationships are more extinct than a gentleman holding a car door open these days.

Reels are favored over videos because they're quick, short, and easily accessible.

People love the highlights.

Picture perfect images of marriages and parenting life are great, as long as the challenging chapters don't come into social accounts to play.

Let's change this I say.

Strength and improvements come with challenges each day;

Damn, I hope that eventually one will just stay.

DRIVING BY (HAIKU IV)

Greetings are in store.
We cruise over in our car
Hello from afar!

GETTING SHARPER

It's probably pre-destiny, or at a minimum it's my somehow earned or meant-to-be future.

My sharpie and I collaborate on yet another day of fresh variations to long lost thoughts.

I desire to be sharper with each new morning alarm.

With a fresh cup of coffee and pen in hand, the hope is there that a break through awaits.

The minutes tick and the hours click, but my mind winds even faster than the time.

My stomach goes from settled to sour.

My heart goes from rhythmic thumping to faded anxious bumping.

I push through and away from the pain.

Encouragement shouts at me in the mirror.

Good riddance yesterday.

Hello, today!

TWO SONS

I helped give you life, but you saved mine.
Pookie is the giver of life and a bright one at that.
Your intelligence, competitiveness, and gentlemaness is inspiring and utterly tremendous.
G is a bold warrior and a one of a kind at that.
Your creativity, resilience, and loving nature is treasured and super admirable.
To my two sons: your too talented and beyond loved to miss the opportunities awaiting you with the thousands of warm, welcoming suns in your promising futures.
Much love forever...

BOOK OF BOURBON

Whiskey drenched pages...
capturing attempts to be courageous.
Judgements pile up more with age...
just like oak barrels season at each stage.
The bottle opens up with a twist...
an open invite for a night's tryst.
Sometimes it lends itself to peace and quiet...
while other times it welcomes a mindful riot.
Each sip allows for a brief relief...
a time to contemplate every belief.
Bourbon beckoned stories bring about laughs and pure joy...
the pages below the sweating low ball glass appear to play coy.
Another sun sets with intentions...
I looked to the comments, but didn't notice any mentions.
Cold, lonely, and dark light fills the room as it pours through the blinds...
In these instances is where the book and my bourbon typically binds.

VERSUS YESTERDAY

Competition encourages new heights of skill, fight, and desire.

Your greatest self is yet to be unlocked by a challenger with a similar spirit.

When life is up and down with ebbs and flows, the best life hack is to avoid wasting away chasing one doe or singular foe.

With that said, I'm squaring up.

It's me today versus me yesterday.

There's many reasons I share these verses, but a huge one is that it's me today versus me yesterday.

Am I a better version today?

I'm not backing down.

My name means "little King" and I'm acting accordingly by getting up and wearing my crown.

PILLOW STREAMS

Every so often I make the unplanned trip to a well known spot to drop off a load of feeling distraught.

Experiencing "loud thoughts of emotional silence" eventually adds up to my emotional outbursts of too long silenced thoughts.

My pillow floods with streams of oversized and watered down pain droplets that finally explode.

Like a pressurized can that's top is finally popped, I share a sacred moment or two with myself.

Bottle it up is what I've learned from cultural indoctrination.

Yes, I'll forever be a tough male and father of two more.

Creating a river from my feelings won't last long though as I jump to design a bridge to walk right over it in no time.

There's no doubt I'll visit this place again.

Until then, be true and keep this between you and me.

Here's to more dreams than streams.

YIPPEE (HAIKU V)

Yippee yelled the king
Two heads are better than one
and six legs are fun

BUT, WHY?

I could rattle off a list of things.
My "why's" adjust from time to time.
However, there's been one why that hasn't left since 2007 regardless of time or space.
Some days that "why" got me up and pushed me to even drink or eat.
Then another unwavering "why" joined that "why" in 2016.
Two is better than one they say.
Undeniable and unconditional love...
Love that you'd die for;
better yet, love that you'd live for.
At times, when I'm simply not my best and not enough to be my own "why"... they are my "why's."
Forever branded into my skin;
Permanently etched into my heart;
They're more than just kin;
They're my "why's" right from the start.

GIVE IT TO ME

No questions or mistakes here.
It's a request versus a plea.
Give me forgiveness for being me.
It's certain you'd want the same.
Go on and drop your stones.
No perfection here, now or never.
What's wanted by both of us is actually the same.
Peace, love, and a bright future exists.
Give me my flowers like I gave you yours.
Now exists, but tomorrow or forever may end up never.
Love was given and I want you to keep it.
Try and deny it, but the King can be the superior witness.
For every mistake, misstep, misspoken word, give me forgiveness.
On second thought, choose to or don't.
Your decisions will never decide what me and my King will or won't.

988

I thought about killing me.
Then I realized that killing me wouldn't kill that which I couldn't.
So I decided to let it be.
I looked up to the best ever.
I thanked Him for my life.
I praised Him for the endeavor...
regardless of seemingly relentless strife.
Thanks for listening to my ideation...
in spite of all my fortunes.
Hey; hand me some libations.
Now let's count up our portions!

DISTURBING NIGHTS

Tossing and turning on a nightly basis...
It's par for the course and completely expected; not necessarily accepted.
Dreams are nightly morphing into nightmares.
Jolting around my king sized bed in cold sweat as my subconscious thoughtfulness is morphing into ironic, lonely upheaval.
Whispers of past victories tease their way in and interrupt my R-E-M.
False hope is quickly ousted as visions of uncommitted lovers spewing words of wrathful disgust enter the scene.
Sleeping in peace is a long lost fantasy that I yearn to rekindle my relationship with.
Day in and day out;
Around and around we go;
Night in and night out.

TURN YOUR FROWN UPSIDE DOWN (HAIKU VI)

During chaotic times
Stubborn frowns are overcome
And turned upside down

PEACEFUL DAYS

Not much compares to the whirring of a breezy fan.

Capturing the nearly complete silence is something rare to cherish.

A nearby ice cube pings the glass as it slowly melts and plops into the glass half full.

Flowing laughter in the distance brings a grin.

For a blip in time, all is well and positivity abounds.

Plants breathe new life and air throughout the space we temporarily occupy in this piece of the mandala.

Peace realized is peace earned and appreciated.

Days and days to come but there's not a one quite like this one.

Give Thanks... Much love

BURNING ALIVE

Blazing rays of sunshine beam down on my story filled skin.

The nearby path is set on fire...

and sizzles as a warning to those who dare to set foot on it.

Relentless gas has come to rule the desert for the summer.

Pools of cool blue water juxtapose the blurry orange, white, and gray hues of heat-infused air that hover the ground.

Only the determined overcomers and finest of evolution makeup will survive this treacherous environment until next season.

Water comforts the creatures seeking respite and liquid gold for the body, mind, and soul.

Splashing around reinvigorates with a blatant reminder that fortunes do exist for the observant opportunists who see and take them.

Greatness exists in spite of recognition or past stories preceding present gratefulness.

STOP AND SMELL THE FLOWERS

We've all earned our flowers.
To many, we'll be a nameless face.
For some, we posses super powers.
Everyone deserves just a bit of grace.
At some point, there's a stumble or fall.
There's plenty of moments to celebrate although sometimes it hurts to go from running back to a crawl.
Life in the big city will teach us to grow.
In one area, we may graduate.
Simultaneously, another area may irritate and frustrate.
Enjoy it and continue the climb.
In the end, true love will see us.
The true love lens sees past the sins and flaws.
We have to be fearless and ferocious.
Believe in yourself like you once did Santa Claus.
Celebrate when graduations are reached for you and yours.
That's what I did today as G passed the K.
Each graduation leads to unlocking new doors.
Take the flowers you've earned today.

BLOOM (HAIKU VII)

Nestled in this pot
Not wondering why this spot
I give into growth

THE COMING LIGHT

Creaking noises as loud as jack hammers torment my head.

The creaking grows seemingly louder and louder with each extra deep inhale and exhale of my body.

Feeble attempts are given to realign my perspective as devil inspired clouds relentlessly attack my damaged pieces.

Realizing the creaking is coming from my insides, I rush to fight for what's left of myself.

My heart and soul cracks and bends while my mind works overtime to prevent from breaking.

A little transcendental meditation allows for brief treaty as I survive to fight another day.

In the depths, there's a spark.

Amidst the dark, there's a flame.

The faint flame provides hope of fire.

For every fire, there was once just a spark.

CONSUMED

Trucks galore and planes that soar.
Materials abound and fill the cargo spaces of rushing transportation modes.
As each order is fulfilled, a hundred more seem to be submitted and billed.
The people just can't get enough as closets, pantries, and living rooms overflow.
Satisfaction is fleeting and the chase continues to satisfy desires that are insatiable.
From west to east and every where in between, items are relocated with great hopes for perfect everlasting matches between good and consumer.
Debts soar and retirement funds dip, but we move on chasing lifestyles obsessed over and peddled by influencers and elitists.
By the way, that reminds me that I just got notified my iPhone 15 bill is overdue.
BRB...

PLANTED

A girl once gifted me a plant.
The gift was for my birthday.
It was a sweet sentiment as she commented that the plant could grow with me.
The girl stayed for a while before exiting on her own growth journey.
My plant is thriving and is a breath of fresh air.
Its roots continue to spread mirroring the labyrinth that is our lives.
We dig down deep searching for the ideal conditions to thrive.
Progressing up the hierarchy of needs, enduring slides back down it, and gripping on with all our might at times.
We root, grow, wilt, die, bloom, adapt, spread out, and endure.
Like plants, we've been gifted a life to journey through with those who join us and care for us.

THIS AND THAT

This and that;
Tit for tat;
Spit and spat.
On and off;
Scoff for cough;
Loss and prof.
It's the way of the loved one.
Those who know us most intimately inflict the most pain and also bring us the most joy.
Tears and fears;
Smiles for cheers;
Frowns and beers.
In and out;
Smirking doubt;
Around and about.
So many life teachers to thank.
Amazing loved ones and rock solid friends too!
Here's a loving smile to them and a straight faced nod to each turnabout intimate partner.

CHURNING (HAIKU VIII)

My stomach is churning
Meanwhile, my mind is yearning
Blue skies are turning

GHOSTED

Look me right in the eyes.
See me when you spill your words.
Catch a full shot of my soul
as you gaze into my windows.
Connections are made that can't be withdrawn or clipped to edit the narrative.
Synapses that travel through time forever and ever have synapsed.
Don't turn your head as you unravel a spool of carefully contrived nonsense to nonchalantly
utter to me.
It's already too late as you peer into the cold distance.
We both know your commitment has ghosted us.
This love was but just seasonal.
I'm certainly not all seeing and will never be all knowing.
Boy, this was just another bad showing.

MINDING YOUR OWN

Mind over matter they say...
Every day is a choice of perspective.
Being proactive with it is key.
Otherwise, suddenly you lose track.
Taking back your attitude is powerful.
Grab a mouth full of positivity and thanks.
Forget shanks and recall some wins.
Transformation will ensue.
Everything blue can actually be used for good.
You'll withstand and get stronger.
No longer giving negativity time or space within your brain matter will make a shift.
Mind your own energy and speak some affirmations.
Wonderful days are here for the taking.

WANTED

Here's a toast to the many we memorialize today.
Give God thanks that I didn't lose one in combat.
Friends and family that I love have less to say.
My respects leave me feeling a way about that.
This day is nothing I earned, but something we all wanted.
Not wanted like Wyatt Earp, but wanted like a single dad giving his all for his young lad.
Today is something that can't be fronted.
Give thanks for all and the true story that shit isn't bad.
Peace and vibes on the home front.
You know when you're getting got and when you're rewarded.
For at least today, we're definitely not shorted.

MEMENTO MORI

Remember your mortality.
It's cemented in history.
We'll forever be immortalized.
Our impact will carry on;
Always and indefinitely.
Blood lines have been altered.
Communities and teams shape shifted.
It's done and it's continuing on.
What's undone is available for doing.
We move to do even better.
We strive for resilience like a water bear.
There's so much to learn about adaptation as I envy the ways of the tardigrade.
Tomorrow's going to come... for some.
Have joy for the golden sunrise.
Leave the past in the burnt sunset.
A Memento Mori is there to be noticed.
Let's be grateful for another page in our story.

HEART

As my youngest likes to say,
My heart is beeping faster and faster.
These type of days bring realization into play of all that is well.
My heart has not been deleted.
The Lord has ensured my soul still isn't depleted.
Bumping of life flows through my chest and there's a rebirth ensuing.
Every additional thump catapults me into the moment and I emphatically announce my arrival.
Arrival to the now, to my space, to my nearby partners in crime who open their arms and minds to the vitality that we share.
I acknowledge life and engage with it as the burning of the hottest commodity in existence ticks away with each deliberate movement of the second hand.

HEART STOPPER (HAIKU IX)

Looks and vibes to kill
Over the top heart stopper
Left me a health bill

THAT 2023 LOVE

Love is a like.
Like is a hug.
A hug is a connection.
Connection is bonding.
Bonding is trusting.
Trusting is truth.
Truth is honesty.
Honesty is care.
Care is unselfish.
Unselfish is giving.
Giving is a love language.
Language is kind words.
A kind word is sweet.
Sweetness is a summer kiss.
A Summer kiss is time together.
Time together is commitment.
Commitment is fleeting these days.
These 2023 days are symbiotic.
That 2023 love is no love lost.
Can't we do better?

MIND FULL

Monsters under his bed are not unlike monsters in my head.

Both fantastical and of imaginative sources.

He reassures me of the pleasures and happiness in life while I reassure me that there's still a kid inside me.

Ok ok I also reassure him of his safety, love, the practice of sharing space, resources, and growth conversations.

Monsters are real if you acknowledge them and non existent if you dismiss them as created foes.

Big furry googley-eyed creatures of dark mass and sharp teeth or small nagging gnats of doubts and criticism just the same.

Monsters in his nightmares are not too unlike negative projections cast onto me over time.

If accepted as truth, they can torment and destroy us while distracting our focus from beautiful flourishing flowers.

Together we can unlearn bad seeds that have blown into our consciousness and embrace new affirmations that lead to self love, security, and acceptance.

My son's monsters are not too unlike mine if you think about it.

ROLLERCOASTER

Sometimes you're the cat.
Sometimes you're the cat lady.
You could be the windshield today and maybe the bug tomorrow.
Life's a rollercoaster.
I've been chasing cat since I was young.
What I've found is that often when you're chasing, you aren't able to be chased.
Until you call off that dog in you, what you're looking for might not come looking for you.
It might make you feel mad, but in reality it isn't that bad.
Consider waiting to be discovered.
No matter your level of want and passion, I'll tell you that cat doesn't come just because of sheer will or desire for it.
It may come to you with the setting sun.
It could leave with the darkness of midnight.
It's unscheduled and untamed.
It's quite frankly a ride that's unnamed.
There's ups, downs, screams of joy, and also of terror.
It's like a rollercoaster.
Just reach high into the sky.
"Look, no hands Ma"
Enjoy the ride!

SWIPE (HAIKU X)

Swipe while the time's right
Embrace while the moment's ripe
Go with what feels right

BLENDED

In this sphere full of green land made up of mostly water that's mixed together with salt, ancient rock, and yet to be discovered life forms...

The human race loves to blend.

It's chameleon like...

fading into environments.

We're not so unlike animals such as zebras, tigers, and cheetahs...

with patterns meant to disguise.

Our personalities are whipped together like fruit smoothies.

They're formed from the raw experiences of life combined with genetic concoctions from our Creator himself.

Each component brings unique backgrounds.

When Individually compared, the dichotomous nature of each element is awe inspiring.

Together, it's a harmonious symphony of meant to be-ness.

Yin and Yanging like soul mates.

Purpling royalty is born from yellow and green donors of destiny.

A palette of finely tuned and carefully chosen pigments brings about a walking, talking, breathing marvel.

Just as good needs evil, gorgeous sunrises and enamoring sunsets need one to have the other.

Doors can't be opened if they aren't first closed.

Around and around we go blending and pretending and bending the truth that we somehow aren't the sum of all our components...

a fluid recipe that's a one of one.

CALL ME WHAT YOU WANT

Call me what you might!
Please don't just due to spite.
Though I thought absent paternity
Might have led to unholy matrimony,
I loved you like you've never ever felt.
I was committed more than your pops was to his half of the DNA that he dealt.
I'm sitting here reaping his and your mom's sown seeds.
Why am I fighting to keep you or earn you with good deeds?
Pomp and circumstances limo tint your sacred veil.
In another life there's no chance this would've ended with a fail.
For better or for worse was not something I wanted redacted.
Even though I'm not perfect, I really think you might've overreacted.
A few days or weeks is actually pretty minuscule.
In the grand scheme of things, I thought you were fire, but you used me as fuel.
One day you might say R I P to at least some of them while my love is still free.
If not, I may just let you be because your liberty means more than for you and I to just agree.
Call me what you may.
I tried my best to keep this at bay.
I'll collect all your insults and bury them in a deep ass whole in my backyard.
Then I'll drink a bourbon and accept the label of try hard...
even though nothing was ever posed.
It was just a well of love that led to what was proposed.

TRUE STORY

An inconvenient truth it might be,
but verbally it's a Fernando Tatis home run;
with spiraling tendencies.
Fact is that we've all been tossed out...
Tossed aside like roaches gathering in the dark together.
Like a golden knight, we're all a little misfit.
Fact is that we've all been passed up;
un-coveted in the least bit.
Bleeding scarlet red from the inside out,
we're all a little Runnin' Rebel.
Fact is no matter what your level, there's always someone that's beyond it.
You may get fired for the next best.
Don't stress as it's just another test.
Fact is that someone else is always lined up.
We've all been replaced and traded before;
as if the grass is always greener.
Fact is that I know this isn't making anyone elated.
It's just an inconvenient truth...
and a vital silver lining reminder to stop and enjoy the journey.

NOT FORGOTTEN

Let me make an effort to elucidate on spun webs of facts that led to this innateness.
Comfortably, I hang on to the vortex...
riding the waves of peace and love...juxtaposed by past trips down regretful lane.
I reside in the power of believing that affirmative reinforcements of bright memories will drown the gutter experiences of nightmare's past.
I refuse to leave true love forgotten.
I'm embracing the challenge to move on from rotten moments and replace the negative words with smiles and pictures of successful triumphs.
I better locate my lucid dream of true love...
invite it to the surface and offer it a permanent lease in my head.
Allow it to spread.
A stage 5 diagnosis of peacefulness is the aggressive goal I seek.
Reaching the peak is not too out of reach...
especially considering each of our thoughts are controllable and our soul is able to guide us on our own self love highway.

FORMING YOU

It's the way that you move forward
and how you do or don't look back.
Forming you is reliant on this and meets at the intersection with Mother Nature.
It's all about getting through and taking steps toward future you...
simultaneously opening the door for lessons learned from reflections of the past.
Forming you is a part creator job and a part you career.
It's an inside job left up to the daily exertion of thoughts on the now...
partnered with the balance of growth through past fires.
Forming you is commanded by the owner of the potter's hands...
who is both the creator and you.
You're the journey man, the front man, the firefighter, the lover, the peace builder, your own
best friend, your greatest teacher, and your one life partner.
Contours of the path are subjected to your own guided discovery and the remnants you leave.
Forming you is a lifelong mission that won't ever reach accomplished status.
It's a road to take in and it's waiting for your toiling to come to fruition.
You are life and life is you.

STICKIE NOTES (HAIKU XI)

Small posted treasures
They're more than just kind gestures
Gifted love measures

ARTISTIC EXPRESSION

Art is an immersive experience.
It's one that can't be defined by dollars and cents.
Imaginative figures dance from one's brain onto canvas.
They take life alongside words of intent and emphasis.
Colors are strewn from edge to edge in harmonious partnership.
Thoughts that were previously concocted in the artist's mind are transferred to paper drip by drip.
Words tango to tell a story as the lines run into one another.
It's an interpretive dance that requires the reader to uncover.
Forms of art are numerous and beyond the limitations of any individual mind.
Soaking in each picture, mold, story, shirt design, song, or building is an experience that's one of a kind.
I have so much love and adoration for every artist and their own endeavor.
May your creativeness flow and the interpreters be clever!

TIME TRAVELS AND TRAVELS AND TRAVELS

It was something long ago that I might've told you...
before ever thinking I may eat crow.
I'm my own worst enemy sometimes,
and I've been around since eighty five.
I'm also all I have besides these crimes.
You should be arrested for hooking me
with all that fake bullshit that took my times.
You robbed me from what I could be.
Sadly I let you rob my years.
I was raped and extorted.
I was left with nothing but smoke and mirrors.
It's not the first and maybe not the last.
You crossed my path and terrorized me.
We burned that path into pieces and since left it in the past.
Time travels and travels and travels
as every tonight marks one less left.
Eventually judgement will reign down with heavy gavels.

ROSES
ARE RED

Violets are blue.
Emotions are rainbow.
Cerebral thoughts are opaque.
Past is black and gray.
Future is brightly lit.
Sunsets are fire.
Sunrises are placid.
Family is set.
Friends are formed.
Thoughts are fluid.
Facts are in stone.
Trying is almost.
Doing is action.
Sadness is a state.
Happiness is a mindset.
Picking is choosing.
Not choosing is losing.

RED ROSE AROSE (HAIKU XII)

Persistent seeds below
Will always find ways to show
What's inside will grow

CHOOSING TO BELIEVE

God has me.
God has the kids.
We will be...
Better place some bids...
Finer than before...
With what He has in store.
Devil thinks he runs it.
Boy is he mistaken.
We will flourish from the pit...
Grow and awaken...
Move differently than ever...
Reach to be more clever.
Lord, I won't quit.
Lord has us.
We won't forget...
That often a negative is a plus...
When things don't seem to add up...
Thank Him for this full cup.
I've never been buried.
But I sure have been planted.
Only burdens that I ever carried...
I gave them to you, granted...
I laid them at your feet...
Pray that one day we'll meet.

SMALL TALK

The words came out "I don't care."
I responded with a genuine long stare.
Wishing that more people did;
Like back when I was just a kid.
How on Earth did we get to this point?
I'm starting to question if it's even the same joint.
You can miss me with all that hate...
Fake headlines and all the click bait.
I love a deep and true conversation;
One that at least leaves the station.
Let's train our youngest ones to talk a bit.
Don't you think that would be lit?
Use some manners and formulate some words...
It's something that's not for the birds.
Listen, I know that I digress.
It's possible that I carry too much stress.
Catch me inside or outside.
Let's talk and not hide.
Except you that used that block feature...
You're not my type of creature!
True story;
You're no longer my worry.

WISHING SWELL

It's on that day that I fell...
Reaching for a dime in the well.
Wound up off balance...
Ended with you closing the valance.
Shaded from the outside...
In darkness we could confide.
Amongst quarters, nickels and pennies...
I reached and said oh geeze a dime; it must be my time!
Some are out there looking for clout...
I couldn't care less what you're all about.
I'm interested for sure as I'm dedicated to the stir.
Pots of experience offer poetic lines, but sometimes I can't see the tree amongst the pines.
Water wells of wishes often appear delicious, particularly in a pond of so many fishes.

FADED NO

No
No time
No time left
No time left to
No time left to give
No time left to give anymore
No time left to give any more
No time left to give any more pieces
No more timepieces left to give any?
Left no time to give any more pieces
Left no time to give any more
Left no time to give anymore
Left no time to give
Left no time to
Left no time
No time
No

TITLE IT

I wish upon a star
to never hear a line so weak...
So weak ever again.
I'll throw my cookies if it's uttered.
"I'll always do this" will give me the fits.
Because "no matter what" leads to what matters.
Words are super cheap...
something that most don't keep.
"What are we" leads to what actually were we?
Uncertain if there's ever a forever...
but I obstinately reclaim my hope.
It's the best way to move on and cope.

INDEPENDENCE (HAIKU XIII)

Red white and blue hues
Pew pew into the night skies
United in joy

POPS

Dedicated
Unwavering
Ethical
Godly
Loyal
Comedic
Athletic
Brave
Leader
Kind
Mannerly

Honest to a tee; a person I always longed to see; someone I wished to be. Alas, he'll always be a part of me.

MOM

Loving
Sweet
Beautiful
Intelligent
Loyal
Caring
Passionate
Hardworking
Spiritual
Relentless
Victorious

One of a kind she'll always be; a person who means the most to me; someone who taught me everything to a degree. Ultimately, there's no one better I could ever foresee

READER

I thought about you.
I prayed for you.
I talked to God about you the other day.
Come one, come all.
Take in this story.
At times it's glory and others it's gory.
It's unapologetically mine.
Share yours too; I won't mind.
One guarantee is that it's truth you'll find.
I'm loving you for sharing in my journey.
These thoughts have been burning.
I needed you to indulge me.
I'm just glad I finally loved me enough to divulge thee.

EVERYBODY SCATTER

So many out here are getting fatter and sadder.
Everybody's scattered.
Isn't it wild how we gather by the masses on select days?
Then everybody scatters.
We convene for weddings, holidays, and church plays.
Then everybody scatters.
We retreat to our respective caves one by one without even being phased.
Everybody scatters.
We live amongst single servings, split homes, and eight seat SUV's for one.
Still everybody scatters.
Scheduled hangs result in military style briefings with short discussions as we come together.
Then we scatter.
We gather somewhere cool to connect, but we simply stare at our personalized devices.
Then we scatter.
Our love is expressed and shared on many levels until evil devils intercede.
Everybody scatters.
We hide our next moves and separate our lives when before we were once wives, husbands,
and sons under one roof.
That was before everybody scattered.
It's like we eventually forgot what mattered amidst all the clatter...
before we prioritized our selves
and everybody scattered.

COME TO

Speak freely like what your words are matter.
It's time that you come to.
Let go of what you thought was coming to you.
Open arms to what you've come to
and thank the world for it all too.
Won't someone else be compelled to share a word or two?
It's my wish to help someone else tell their tale too.
It's our time to come to.

VAULT

You picked the lock while I was unguarded and opened the vault and picked up the pieces.
You need to be careful what you handle.
Some pieces are hot as shit and others are arctic cold.
How long until you fold and lock it all back up?
Or are your plans to handle with care and see how we fair?
It's not a dare, but it's tough now that you see what I bare.
There's no checks inside this vault so how's it feel?
I'm not in the mood or the shape to make a deal so why don't you just go.

STYLED (HAIKU XIV)

Mild but sometimes wild
No doubt I'm uniquely styled
Is it fit check time?

NON FICTION

Shoved in between the intro and the references page is a story that can only be seen by reading between the lines.
The contents of the story provide all the pretenses to the present.
Future versions and sequels rely on dramatic prequels with detailed facts and articulated experiences.
Peer into the center pages and discover the lost words of an author whose life has only been minimally told.

IT'S MORE

It's more than just your whit.
It's every tid bit and how you stay on your shit; intensified by your charm and your desire to never harm.
Your words are backed up by actions like a perfectly concocted pudding full of proof within it.
This leads me to want to treat you like royalty and give you all of my loyalty.
Attention to detail is minor when it entails showing care to you and all that you bare.
My mind's eye is opened to future celebration of two brains and all the earned gains from efforts to fulfill and satisfy both heads.
Your "for reals" gives me all the damn feels.

RABBIT HOLE

Earth spins around and around as we drowned ourselves in puddles...
small shallow obstacles amidst the course of life.
Lulled to sleep by the continuous rotation and circular motion...
awakening over and over from the most recent moonlit slumber.
We move forward in slow motion as we continue down the rabbit hole.
There is no toll but the one we charge ourselves during our contemplation of this conundrum.
With all the inflation it's no wonder we don't all blow up and show up in the after realm together.
Forever and ever we continue down this rabbit hole...

BENDING WITH THE WIND

I got flustered and made an adjustment.
I decided to give up the luster of the past and embrace the future of the now.
It's amazing just how quickly priorities can change and be exchanged for new ones.
I lost tons of things and embraced new flings to see what new life brings.
I lost so many titles but agreed that they're
simply something that only matters to entitleds.
Bending in new directions;
regardless of imperfections;
no more lectures desired and you can also keep your conjectures.
I'm living life until the end and open to what's around the bend.
All the other nonsense can float in the wind...

LET IT COME

Working on not working on it.
When the coming and goings slow,
the flow transitions to a low pressure drip.
It's time to flip the script and open the crypt of story telling follies.
When it's not coming to me, I'm going to it.
I'm showing that it can be created and that words in tandem with other words can't be understated.
With each meaning, the time is feening for a new piece of perspective that can prove to be effective and forward leaning.

PAINTING (HAIKU XV)

Experimenting
Zig and zag and dip and dab
Painting in the lab

UNANTICIPATED SWELLS

No expectations for greatness...
just gratefulness for everything.
Give thanks for lateness...
things come in divine timing.
Often, there's no obvious rhyming...
there's no clear reasoning.
Unanticipated swells of grace and gifts...
paralleled by dips of faith and increased fits.
Let go and let flow...
A sea of life is present!

THUNDEROUS BLUE SKIES

Amidst the incoming blue skies, there's thunderous rumblings of lies to old ties.

Blue hues of brightness taint angry bursts of the few dark clues left unnoticed.

Shape shifting skies travel faster than the sifting sands and good byes of the prior night's eyes.

Could this be a clearing or a new something worth fearing?

GOOD NEWS

She's my good news delivered on junk day.

She's the one that no matter what I know she's got my back.

With her, my home, my life, and everything is on track... even with all that I lack.

It's irrelevant what I'm lacking because she's backing me.

Together, we are packing.

We're off to new destinations and untraveled places to visit God's creations.

I'm so grateful for the trials and tribulations that brought me to this.

Good news is here and the rest is into the abyss.

PEACE (HAIKU XVI)

My head's in the clouds
I'm dreaming of peace that abounds
Peace larger than life

FORGET WHAT I TOLD YOU

I want to show you what I feel,
but everyone knows that's not that the deal... because you can't see what you feel.
Or can you?

LOCKED

Have you ever enjoyed an endeavor?
An endeavor that locked all future levers.
And destroyed other forevers?
Felt so good to untether;
And she was so inanely clever.
She grabbed what was hers
and found the shit that endures.
They said "just cut it out" and it left a hole of doubt about what life is all about.
When it comes to being strong, it's been a project that's life long.
My love runs so deep for those that I choose to keep.
My entire heart and soul is given because I'm driven to be whole.
Life with you is complete and I really want me to be the one you take deep.
Goals are semi steep, but I'm ready for the leap.
You're the whole to fill my empty mole that was cut from deep below and left me feeling low.
Take my hand and my soul and tie it with your bow.

NOTHING LESS

Streaming the game like an epic play in life will make the top ten.
Yearning to equip myself with the skills to make the starting squad.
Looking to my closest pod to sharpen me with love and desire.
Hoping that they unlock the fire for the things we all desire.
Peace love and happiness and nothing less.
Meet me in the middle and let's share the ingredients that impress.

LEARNING

Emotional words beget undesigned nights leading to shocking frights.

No amount of hurt can be simply erased as I continue on to create new challenges yet to be faced.

Regrets build up because I compound mistakes and amplify hurts that abound.

Digging deep to pursue more days, but I just keep noticing more and more grays.

My hair is turning and my stomach's churning from all this learning.

God is waiting for me to hit rock bottom and then he may just say got 'em.

Here we go...

Moving on from yet another low.

UNWANTED PROFESSORS

Years ago my capstone project was aced. Yet, the "professors" are still crazed up in my face.
They're illegitimate, self proclaimed, and completely untamed.
Know-it-alls rushing to grade my papers.
Then the love tapers.
Pots yell at kettles for being black.
It's like everyone wants a crack, and very few have your back.

FOREVER BOND (HAIKU XVII)

Mountains and Mountains
We've ventured far and beyond
A forever bond

HELLO COULD'VE BEEN ENOUGH

A first kiss was followed up with a goodbye.
Alas, it didn't end there as fate might have allowed.
Instead it carried on and went off the cuff.
Each day contained another additional sigh.
Finally, all the peace and happiness was drained.
No regrets to give.
But, it couldn't hello been enough?
Better yet, a hello ending with a quick blissful kiss.
Why'd it have to lead to all of this?

TO MY BRIDE TO BE

I don't want today to slide without expressing how much you mean to me.
Something that I must confess is that I'm yours and really nothing less.
Our days on Earth are numbered and I wish them all to be with you.
I really really do.
Your smile, kiss, and heart are just a few things that I never want to be apart.
Fate is ours forever.
Know that you and I are here to stay and forever it will be that way.

WARRIORS

Faint cheers of victory rang throughout my skull of dichotomous thoughts and emotions.
My desire to out last was concreted because being defeated was not an option.
Summoning inspiration from fictional characters was not off the table.
I've always been able to enable manifestations that have led to success.
The subconscious first thought may be unmanageable at times, but the conscious has always fought the second.
With a cloud of gratefulness and the protection of faithfulness, I open my heart and grab my script to play my part.

UNITED (HAIKU XVIII)

United we cruise
The wheels stay in full motion
Freedom we wont lose

KING ME

King sized thoughts slip through the air.
I'm challenged to acknowledge each one and then push it away.
King sized beds provide consistent nights of restlessness.
The comings and goings of life's inner dialogue are put to rest and then revived over and over again.
King sized candy bars attempt to coat the stomach in false comfort.
Sugar coated one liners of positivity and encouragement await morning's sunrise.
King sized promises of everlasting life echo in the deep chambers of gold plated memory vaults.
Receptacles nearby whine as they overflow with the remnants of today's unwanted garbage.
King sized meals from brown paper bags are snatched from tiny portholes by passers by in the night searching for another insatiable feeling that's inevitably being handed over.
We know not what destination awaits on the other side of this enigmatic dream world.

PURGATORY STORY

Working on the staircase that I currently face...
Looking to climb out of the latest hole that I fell into.
Upwards is the motion and forward with devotion...
Not enough shakes exist to satisfy what my head can't fathom persists on Earth.
From the dust we came and to the dust we'll return.
Meanwhile, in purgatory it's a must to seek His glory.
Feeling beyond grateful, even for the hateful, because it's all in the cards.
I'm never forsaken and He's always making a hand that ultimately wins.

WHO

2 times was too many for me to allow before having an epiphany.

4 months in and it felt like the pen, but without the gin.

6 episodes deep, but it felt like I was a main character in the wrong series.

8 fully blown months led to knowing that grown beings should sometimes reap what's been sewn on their own.

Now it's time to ask: who do you appreciate?

EVOLVING

How many of you said that this man has changed?
If you thought I was going to remain stagnant, then we all know who's really deranged.
There's way too many people running around two fanged.
It wasn't me that you were searching for, but yeah we hanged.
Now remove your claws from my balls as the bells have clanged.
Times up for you and yours because the old me and you are indefinitely estranged.

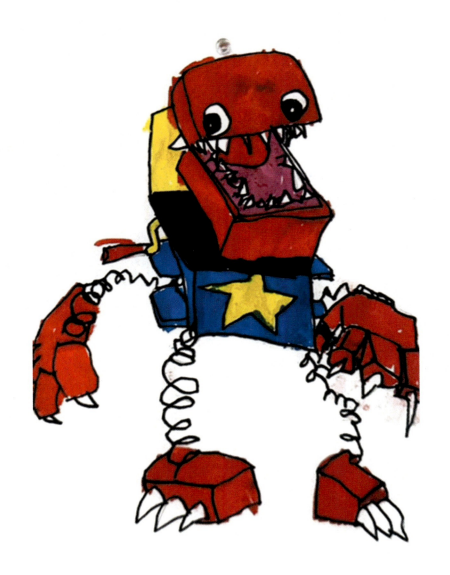

FUTURISTIC (HAIKU XIX)

Morphing into new forms
Gaining characteristics
Future me coming!

2024

Although I might have arrived last, I came to first.
Something burst within my flesh walls.
Great falls led to climbing higher for new perspectives.
The increasing electives bring new energy for the journey ahead.
Victorious ides await for the two four as I
indulge in more learning to endure more.

DESTINED

When you showed up at the spot and saw the Cadillac, you knew I was back.
What you didn't quite understand was the magnitude of my hand.
Jesus did... and I'm grateful to be his kid.
A royal flush was dealt to me and what He wants is what it will be.
Don't gamble against me again as I continue to step into what's within.
With each new day that I wake, it's going to be me and you know who.

FULL SAIL & WILL NOT FAIL

Wind is at my back as I let out all the slack.

It's "me" time so just let me be.

I'm on full sail.

I'm over having a tail and now I'm with having wind at my back.

I'm fully determined to slide into the next version of this flesh and of this text.

Oceans are left to explore and I know I'm meant for so much more.

Check your own map and quit peaking at the compass in my lap.

I've come too far to not go further.

Now's the time to set the bar higher and do more.

YOUR TURN

YOUR NOTES AND DOODLES HERE

YOUR NOTES AND DOODLES HERE

YOUR NOTES AND DOODLES HERE

YOUR NOTES AND DOODLES HERE

YOUR NOTES AND DOODLES HERE

YOUR NOTES AND DOODLES HERE

YOUR NOTES AND DOODLES HERE

YOUR NOTES AND DOODLES HERE

YOUR NOTES AND DOODLES HERE

YOUR NOTES AND DOODLES HERE

ACKNOWLEDGEMENTS

Thank you for reading my words and drinking in the artwork that Gunnar and I have shared with you. This book is my (possibly feeble) attempt to connect with you on a fulfilling, vulnerable, but extremely honest level. I understand this book and this project will live on past our earthly lifetimes and I fully accept my flawed self and the current interpretations and observations of life that is contained within.

I'd like to thank and give all my love to Luke, Gunnar, Mom, Pops, H. Jerome Alexander, Jesus, all my opps, and myself.

Printed in the United States
by Baker & Taylor Publisher Services